ANSWERS
TO THE
STRUGGLES
OF LIFE

BY
DAVID SMITH

B180 Basketball, Inc.
P.O. Box 2406
Midland, MI 48641-2406
www.b180basketball.com
Phone: 1-800-957-1275

©2022 by David Smith. All rights reserved.

No part of this book may be reproduced, stored in a retrieval system, or transmitted by any means without written permission of the author.

Original Publication Date: 5/1/2012
Published by B180 Basketball, Inc. 6/3/2022
ISBN: (sc) 978-1-7325361-7-3
ISBN: (e) 978-1-7325361-8-0
Library of Congress Control Number: 2022908476

Any persons depicted in stock imagery are models, and such images are being used for illustrative purposes only.

Because of the dynamic nature of the Internet, any web addresses or links contained in this book may have changed since publication and may no longer be valid. The views expressed in this work are solely those of the author and do not necessarily reflect the views of the publisher, and the publisher hereby disclaims any responsibility for them.

Contents

Dedication iv

Acknowledgments v

Chapter 1 – Sacrifice 1

Chapter 2 – Self-Fulfillment 9

Chapter 3 – Listening 15

Chapter 4 – Doing What's Right 19

Chapter 5 – Diversity 23

Chapter 6 – Leadership 27

Chapter 7 – Family 31

Dedication

To my father, who has instilled in me leadership, courage, and determination. To my mother, who has walked with and gave me love, laughter, and comfort along my journey. I want to thank you for never giving up and leading by example. To my wife and children I love you.

Acknowledgments

There have been many individuals that have made a difference in my life. I would like to first acknowledge my parents the late David C Smith Sr. & Connie Smith. I was very fortunate to have parents that were married for almost 30 years.

Along with my parents, I have had my grandmother the late Lula Burnise Smith, as well as many uncles, aunts, cousins, coaches, and friends that have made a great impact on my life.

Chapter 1

Sacrifice

"You Have to Give Something to Get Something"

As a teenager I was never really into the most popular fashions. I spent the majority of my time concentrating on the sports I loved; basketball & football. You guessed it, I was a t-shirt and sweat pants type of person. I'd have many opportunities to get most of the types of clothes and shoes that everyone was wearing. This was in part due to my father working and paying for it. My father worked hard all his life. He only had a high school education, but had the mind of a doctoral recipient. There was a span at the beginning of my teen years when my father worked seven days a week and twelve hours a day. This was the only source of income our family had, so he made sure the best he could that most of our wants and needs were met. He worked at this rigorous, physically, & mentally draining pace for most of his life. During this time that he worked, he stressed the importance of being educated, respectful, honest, and hardworking. He also stressed the importance of sacrifice. He explained the sacrifice that he was making to better the generations after he was gone.

He couldn't attend many extra-curricular activities, but he could be there for every holiday. He missed a lot of personal one on one time with me and my siblings because he had to work. There were seven of us and my mother. I was the second oldest and the oldest boy. As I got older, I began to understand more and more about what he was instilling in us. It really didn't matter if we were rich or poor in the end. If you do not prepare the generations that succeed you, you are destined to become extinct. This next generation should be equipped with the knowledge and ethics from you to carry the generation a step further in the future. This all comes from sacrificing. It means giving up something that pleases you for something that may be beneath you, will better the generations after you.

The majority of your life has to be focused on making wise decisions for the generations that come after you. There must be a great example set forth.

If you stay away from drugs & alcohol and stress the effects of its harm to the individual and others around them, it will enlighten the individual when they become exposed to it by others. I don't remember a time in my life when my parents talked about or used drugs in my presence. My father however, did drink alcohol. I think his rigorous schedule and work life caused him to drink. He never let it get the best of him though. He was determined to be a leader by example.

Friends come and go. Some may have different values than you. Some may have the same outlook on life as you, but a different way of doing things. Never let someone influence your own thoughts or actions. You have to be a leader in times when friends are making you choose to be in or out. The majority of the time, it's best to be out. Don't get me wrong, having friends are great, but sometimes you have to sacrifice friendships for the better of your future generations. True friends will understand and always be in your life. I remember as a little boy when my family moved to a new school district. I wanted to stay in my old school district because of the friends I had made. In the new district we moved to, I didn't know anyone. It was a lot different than my old school in part because of the diversity of the students. I was completely open to all races. In return, I made new friends and expanded my knowledge of other races and the world as a whole. I believe everyone should try to obtain a good understanding of other races and cultures to help prepare future generations. I wouldn't have been able to obtain this if I would have stayed at my old school.

Family is another sacrifice that an individual must make. This may be the hardest thing that you can choose to do. All of your hopes and dreams are in front of you. Most of the time a choice has to be made to whether part from your family to reach that dream or not. This journey must be made alone because no one but you knows what your dream or goal means to you. The support may be there but not full hearted because it's not their dream or goal. This does not mean that your family is against you. It just means that no one can be you to feel how passionate you are about your dream, mission, or goal. Family is the most important factor in an individual's life. The members of your family will love you unconditional yet, be your worst critic. In the end, you will eventually be able to maintain a balance between your family and your goals if you learn to understand and believe in both. I remember when I left for college; I was scared, happy, anxious, and heartbroken all at the same time.

I missed my family all the time. I couldn't turn back though. I felt that if I turned back, I would not be able to set a new standard or experience the full outcome of my own dreams and goals while in college. It hurt bad to not have both. My belief was that this would be a stepping stone for the children that I have. Sacrifice comes in many ways. Sacrifice means making a decision that prepares you as well as your family for future harmony. It's like living a puzzle. The puzzle can be formed instantly or slowly. The picture that the puzzle makes depends on the decisions you make along your journey. Many individuals may choose the quick and easy way out. Some may even have success. The underlying message that I want you to understand is that you must go through the storm to experience what you will give to your future generations.

Never pass the torch without giving your whole heart and soul until the end. Living an honest, happy, and complete life may seem difficult. I remember when I became a father.

I was full of emotions similar to how I felt when entering college. I knew that in order for my children to better themselves as well as the generations after them, they would have to experience many things that I didn't as a kid. I wanted to make that possible as well as stress honesty, doing things the right way, and leading with heart and determination. Finally, everyone makes some sort of sacrifice every day. It may be saving money for a pair of shoes, to giving up cigarettes or soda pop for better health. Do you think that sacrificing for the sake of your future family generations is important? If the answer is yes, I encourage you to continue reading this book. We will work together on becoming a complete individual that values honesty, leadership, heart, determination, and commitment. You have to start somewhere so, let's begin today. Success will be there in the end!

Chapter 2

Self-Fulfillment

"Do Exactly What You Want To Do; Catch That Dream"

I can remember dribbling a basketball between my legs up & down the street. I'd do this continuously without making a mistake. I strived every day to be the best in whatever I did. I felt that in order for me to truly understand and admit my own weakness, I had given my best. I then tried to make my weaknesses my strength. Self-fulfillment means completely experiencing everything that you want out of life and being honest along the way. If you are not honest with yourself you can't move forward. As I dribbled that basketball down the street, I was aware that my right hand was stronger than my left hand. I knew that I couldn't look down at the ball or I would walk into the streets and be hit by a car. Many times life is similar to this, you may have to continue trying not to make a mistake, but if you do, you have to be strong enough and have the heart and determination to start over again. All while keeping your head up and improving your weaknesses. As you're experiencing what you want out of life, you should pay attention to every detail. This includes the relationships you build, your daily habits & routines, your thoughts & attitudes towards other people you don't know, your religious understanding, and your overall happiness. Many times I use to wonder why I didn't start reading the bible earlier in life. I have a very good understanding of all other religions as well. As a teenager I remember when I decided to get baptized. I made the decision by myself. There may be times throughout your life that you will want to turn to someone for advice. You probably won't know who to trust either. When you reach this stage, reading your bible from the very beginning to the end, 2 pages one day at a time will help in advising you on what to do. Self-fulfillment is a time when you truly need to be doing exactly what you want to do with your life. If you fail, so what, you have still fulfilled a part of your life that will help in moving your generation forward. Your experiences will help mold not only your children, but also the people you come into contact with throughout your life. However, you have to remember, if life is only meant to fulfill your own personal dreams and goals, then your life will not be complete. Believing that you are needed even when not asked is hard to understand. It may be hard to come back after you feel that you've failed. It will be that moment when you are needed to help others. I know this may seem odd, but give it your absolute best. Like most young boys my age, I had dreams of playing a professional sport. When the time came for me to experience the life of a professional athlete, I understood what it took. I took advantage of the small opportunities I had. As I went through the tryout process, I began thinking more and more about my life as a professional athlete, my wife, children, and other family members. I realized that I would not be able to see my family as much if I was a professional athlete. The dream of being a professional athlete was not as big as being able to create a long-lasting family bond the way that I envisioned it to be. My view of the life of a professional athlete all of a sudden seemed to diminish. Though this is a sacrifice, the underlying problem that I believed was that being away from your wife and children for long periods of time damages the chance to better the generations after you. There may be monetary success and gain, but where it really counts; which is the hearts of the ones that love you. There would be a failure. Self-fulfillment is an important area in your development. Please understand that this stage is a process that must be completed. Be honest with who you are and what it is that you want.

Chapter 3

Listening

"Don't Just Go By What You Believe, See It From Their Point Of View"

I remember when I was about 9 years old. I'd listen to my father and mother discuss the bills they were going to pay with the upcoming check. I couldn't say anything to them about what to do with the money because I didn't know what was owed on each bill and I did not earn an income to help pay a bill. This process was very helpful in my development of listening skills. Parents are the amplifiers of information. This information can be positive or negative based on the integrity of the parent. This is a very important point. How you perceive the world and your reaction to the problems in the world may result in someone else listening to information that is filled with a positive or negative emotional tone. We all were a kid once. The most influential and motivating people in our lives whether good or bad are our parents. Listening is a learned art. It takes a lot of practice. If you are able to listen to a person and truly put yourself in their situation, then you are able to understand their point of view. I'm not talking about a person that listens but zones in and out when another person is talking. Listening and hearing are two different processes. It's similar to saying you love someone when deep down you are not really sure if you do. Being a good listener will enable you to help some of your closest friends as well as your other personal relationships. Most individuals simply want to be heard. They would rather talk than listen. I don't know why it is such, but if you can understand a person from their perspective you will continuously grow as an individual. Life will be full of opportunities to help others. Make sure you take advantage of them. You'll find that the more you give, the more you will get in return. In today's day and age, the use of technology has hindered the art of listening to another person. The rule should be to talk and listen to someone face to face or in person three times more than you interact with them through technology. A simple lunch appointment would work. There was a time when I wasn't a good listener. It seemed like whatever my mother or father would say to me, I'd do the opposite. I never took time to really analyze what they were asking or telling me to do. I also didn't take the time to see things from their perspective. It was all about me. Remember this; being a good listener will help you through all stages of your life—child, teen, adult, parent, and grandparent.

Chapter 4

Doing What's Right

"Most Of The Time It Will Hurt More To Do Things The Right Way"

This may be the hardest thing for a person to do. The world is full of short cuts, easy ways, deceptions, and cheats. If you truly want something, do things the correct way to attain it. This will make attaining it worthwhile. If you choose not to do things the right way and you still obtain your goal, you will always second guess yourself. You will not be able to encourage yourself to do simple daily tasks with your absolute best effort. Therefore, by cheating to win—you really lose over and over again.

I remember running a mile that was timed. In my mind I knew I was going to give my best to be first. I wasn't going to fake like I had a cramp or another injury to get out of running. I wanted to be first and I wanted to have everyone that I was running against to give their best effort. As I began the last lap in the mile run, I remember subconsciously picturing myself coming in with the best time. What I mean by this is that instead of trying to find a short cut or a way to cheat, try picturing yourself in your own mind winning by doing things the right way. Anybody can find a short cut, but very few can continuously picture honest success because it requires hard work. You will have many friends ridicule you because you choose to do what's right. You'll think huh, some friend. It's a choice that you will live with. Just remember, your past and future generations are counting on you.

Doing what's right means opening and closing the door for others, being polite and courteous, saying "hello", 'please", and "thank you". It also means saying no when you have to when everyone else is saying yes. I guarantee that this last one will be a constant battle. Everyday a choice will have to be made. Please choose what's right.

Chapter 5

Diversity

"Let Go Of Your Beliefs To Understand Everyone Around You"

The world is full of many different races, cultures, beliefs, and religions. There is not one greater or lesser than any other. What will make a person unique is the number of different people they actually get to know. I don't mean holding a short conversation with someone while still holding your original perception about the person. I mean really getting to understand the person. This is where your listening skills will help you. As you begin to understand other people, you will begin to grow even more into a complete person. No one can take away the experiences you gain. I don't mean to take on another person's belief or religion. I mean just truly respect and understand them from their perspective and way of life not yours. You will still be able to have your own view or perspective. Hopefully, they will respect yours.

Diversity has been a part of our world since the beginning of time. Lives are made and ruined based on their decisions about diversity. People are people, if you want to be acquainted with someone who is not like you, it's totally fine. Never listen to outsiders. They are simply telling you what they believe to be true. If you are able to put yourself in their shoes and understand what they have been through in their life, you will be able to understand why they are saying what they say to you. To grow into a complete person, acceptance of everyone must be mastered. It will take time, but remember time goes by fast so change yourself, don't ask the person to change. I remember my first encounter with someone from another country. I was in college. I'd talk to the person as if I knew their language and belief. I really tried to understand the person. My deep down feeling was that this individual had something to teach me. I would not be complete without trying to understand this individual from their perspective. I never looked at the color of their skin, their religion, or where they were from. I actually wanted to learn from each encounter that I had with the person. If you are able to put your own judgments on race and religion aside and never use them as a barrier, you will overcome more obstacles in your lifetime than the majority of the world. Embrace diversity!

Chapter 6

Leadership

"Know Where You Want To Go In Life And Teach Others How To Do The Same"

Being a leader takes so much integrity. You have to be understanding, but aware of the situation, life will never tell you if you are right or wrong until you make your decision. Leaders must plan, have a vision, and maintain their composure. Being able to plan for the expected and unexpected will help you understand what you are about to experience. Having a vision gives you a chance to mentally prepare as well as see the future unfold as you live it. If you are able to maintain your composure during any extreme event, it will prepare you even more to lead. Never let one event or person discourage you. That's life giving you an opportunity to lead the right way. There are many ways to respond to a situation; most leaders respond under control and with a sense of what they are going to do. You have to stay determined to focus on the positives in the situation. If there is no positive, you must think and relate the situation to a positive event that you've experienced. Get a smile out of it some way or another. The definition of leadership can be found in the soul of the person that is doing what is right by God. If a person can give more than they receive, then this will determine if you are on the right path. I remember a time when my friends (who I thought were my best friends at the time) wanted me to do something that I really didn't want to do. Inside I was thinking maybe I shouldn't; then I'd think maybe I should... I chose not to do what they were asking. This decision alone is probably why I'm able to write this book. I was able to grow into a better person after that event. I believe in my creator (God of Abraham). I know that God put me on this earth to help other people. The people I help or inspire will also help others change their decisions and ways of lives to make for better generations to come. You will have to set yourself apart from everyone else. What I mean by this is— knowing when to say yes and no is very important. Always use common sense when deciding. Life can be a great experience if you are able to lead as well as care for others as you care for yourself. Take the time to learn from other leaders along your journey.

Chapter 7

Family

"Understand Everyone- Teach And Learn From Them"

Letting go will be very hard to do no matter how well you prepare. When you lose a family member; the only thing you will think or say is "why". It will hurt very badly. During this low time, other family must be let in to help. Positive environments, actions, habits, and thinking must be experienced daily. I remember when my father passed, I was at work. Something in my mind instantly told me that he was gone. I felt it all over my body. I cried and cried inside and out even though I really didn't know for sure yet. To get through times like this I truly recommend reading your bible or other religious book, trusting and listening to your family members, and giving & showing love to the ones you love most. Remember, the person you lost is going to a better place and has prepared you to deal with this situation over the course of the years he or she was living. Know that the time you spent with them was meaningful and put in place for you to truly learn from them and they like wise learn from you. You probably passed on what you learned to someone else not really knowing that you did. The person you lost will always love you and

I know that you will always love them. Treasure the experience.

There was a time during my childhood when I'd dream about how my life and children would look. I wondered what type of father I'd be. I also wondered if I could handle the role of an adult. It seemed very scary at the time. I remember watching the different types of families that I came into contact with. I would analyze the make-up of the family such as single parent or two parent homes. Some of my friends didn't even have parents. I couldn't imagine life without my parents or siblings. Family should be the building block of all of your dreams. If love, harmony, truth, and faith exists within a family it can withstand almost anything. It takes both parents to trust each other as well as trust their children in all aspects of life happenings. As a family, certain morals and values must be upheld by each of the members. I remember coming home from college and seeing my father wearing some oil drenched pants, a t-shirt, and torn house shoes. I thought to myself, I now understand why? He sacrificed material things to help each family member attain a since of self-worth. He also, unconsciously instilled a value of unselfishness, discipline, and love. This is something that's very hard to do.

As you journey down the path of life I want you to know that whatever road you've chosen to travel; don't look back learn from your past and let the next generation know that you still got it.

In His Own Words

Some things happen for a reason
Like the constant flow of greed through each season.
Life was made to forgive a soul's downfall.
But what is a world if it's not made for all?
As I ponder on life's greatest tasks.
I'm still left with questions that you ask.
You are all the same whether race or creed.
There's still always one common flaw; greed.
Though this problem will continue to exist.
It should occur to you that a life's at risk.
You may be separated by regions and beliefs.
I'm still real to all and those who seek.
Unconditional love and harmony is the answer.
Those who believe will be the ones who prosper.
There may be pains throughout this dance.
A change without knowing gives you another chance.
Holding on to the future is the key to all prayers.
Although yours were answered, don't forget theirs.
These are my words and I believe this to be true.
I know there's a chance, I believe in you.

By David Carl Smith Jr.

NOTES

Write down at least one goal that you want to accomplish in your lifetime.

Goal:

Draw a picture below of you accomplishing your goal.

Picture:

NOTES

Write down at least one goal that you want to accomplish in your lifetime.

Goal:

Draw a picture below of you accomplishing your goal.

Picture:

NOTES

Write down at least one goal that you want to accomplish in your lifetime.

Goal:

Draw a picture below of you accomplishing your goal.

Picture:

NOTES

Write down at least one goal that you want to accomplish in your lifetime.

Goal:

Draw a picture below of you accomplishing your goal.

Picture:

NOTES

Write down at least one goal that you want to accomplish in your lifetime.

Goal:

Draw a picture below of you accomplishing your goal.

Picture:

NOTES

Write down at least one goal that you want to accomplish in your lifetime.

Goal:

Draw a picture below of you accomplishing your goal.

Picture:

NOTES

Write down at least one goal that you want to accomplish in your lifetime.

Goal:

Draw a picture below of you accomplishing your goal.

Picture:

www.ingramcontent.com/pod-product-compliance
Lightning Source LLC
Chambersburg PA
CBHW071917070526
44583CB00016B/2032